An Autopsy Of Us.

D. Leighton

An Autopsy Of Us

Copyright © 2024 by D. Leighton

All rights reserved. No part of this publication may be reproduced, distributed, or transmitted in any form or by any means, including photocopying, recording, or other electronic or mechanical methods, without the prior written permission of the publisher, except in the case of brief quotations embodied in critical reviews and certain other noncommercial uses permitted by copyright law. For permission requests, write to the publisher/author.

I am so happy you're here.

An Autopsy Of Us

This one is for me.
The fire had to burn somewhere.

An Autopsy Of Us

In a world where strength is often defined by how much one can endure without breaking, the notion of vulnerability is frequently seen as a weakness. To peel back the layers of one's soul, to bare the heart openly, is an act of profound bravery and strength. It is in this spirit of courage and raw honesty that *An Autopsy Of Us* was born.

This collection covers hard topics such as assault and abuse, growing up in a larger body, and leaving a dangerous relationship. Please approach these pages with care and compassion, both for yourself and for the stories they hold. Take care of yourself, above all else.

To every reader who has ever loved to a fault, who has sacrificed their own heart for the sake of others, and who continues to rise despite the odds—this collection is for you, too. You survived. That alone is worth celebrating.

May you find solace in these words and may you draw strength from knowing that you are not alone. Embrace your tears as a sign of your capacity to love deeply and feel profoundly, because *that* is beautiful. *You* are beautiful.

Here's to the charms of being human, in all its fragile and fierce glory.

With peace, love, and gratitude,

D. Leighton.

08. Perpetually pleading your case
10. Sacrifice
11. The ghost
12. Keen eye
14. Little one
16. Peach pit
17. I stick around
18. *This is not about money*
20. If I was a worm
21. Moss
22. A crown of serpents
24. Hungry eyes
25. A family heirloom
26. Suck it in
28. Across the sky
29. The thing
30. Bandage
32. Please
33. A wilted rose
34. Oxidized
36. Anthropomorphize
38. She
39. Famished
40. Bare and broke
41. Deaf ears
42. Bloom
44. Not your saviour
45. Fleeing
46. You haunt me
47. Why?
48. What we used to be
50. Fragments
51. Ghosts are stubborn
52. Silence
54. *Oh, right*
55. Aftermath
56. You didn't hit me, you didn't have to
57. A thousand letters
58. Garden of one flower

60. Origin story
61. Someone like me
62. The water
63. Still burning
64. I would be a lot happier if I didn't think
65. The weight of almost
66. Meant to happen
67. This place is not the same
68. Phantom limb
69. When the smoke clears
70. Spilled
74. Consider this my final contribution

An Autopsy Of Us

I find myself
day after day

perpetually pleading your case
to the jury of my mind

as if convincing myself
will erase the hurt you've carved into my bones
the doubt you've sewn into my soul

you didn't mean it
I hope
just a moment of weakness or slip of the tongue

each time I have ruthlessly defended your name
I chip away at my own

drowning in the need to believe
you're still the person I once loved

how many times can I stand
in the courtroom of my being
before the truth demands a verdict?

before I admit that pleading your case
is nothing more than self-betrayal

I am both the accused and the accuser
your defendant and my only witness
torn between justice and mercy
knowing that neither will bring peace

I plead your case with the fervour
of a sinner seeking redemption
a futile attempt to make sense of the pain

the gavel's strike echoes in the emptiness
where your voice should have been.

An Autopsy Of Us

An Autopsy Of Us

I have never needed an excuse
to **sacrifice**
all that I am for other people

I will peel back the layers of my soul
and lay myself bare for you

you don't even have to ask
I am a painfully soft woman
of that I am both proud and ashamed

I gave him pieces of a heart
that I didn't know could break
until he left

and then I glued them back together

carefully

meticulously

just for him to crush it over
and over
and over

So just imagine
all that I could do
will do

for you.

An Autopsy Of Us

You blossomed
under my care

I wilted
from giving too much

you
are the best version of yourself now

and I
am **the ghost**
of what it took to get you there.

An Autopsy Of Us

I've always had a **keen eye**

when I was a kid
I saw castles where they saw sand

a fortress where they saw trees and brush

my dream home in a pile of cardboard and pillows

as a teenager
I saw a scale where there was food
true love where it was only lust
for him at least

friendship when there was lies and betrayal

my friend tell me sometimes a rock is just a rock

i've had to train my eyes to see what is
and is not a geode

but even still
in my peripherals
and my rear view mirror

I get glimpses of what there was

what there is

and what there could be.

An Autopsy Of Us

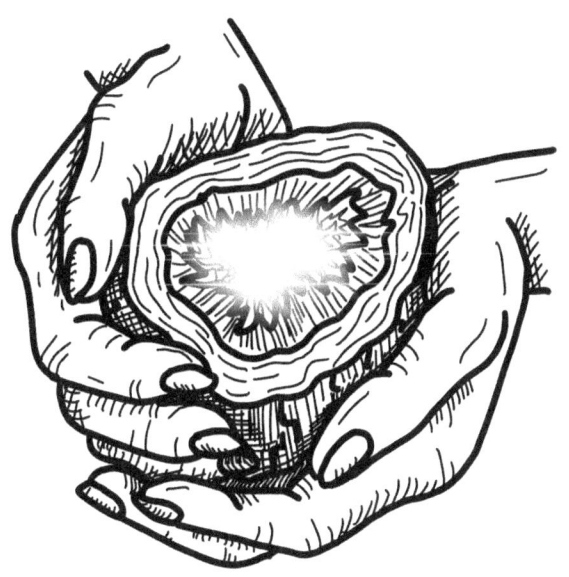

An Autopsy Of Us

you have fallen
little one

your fall broken
only by the weeds

overgrown

through the cracks in my pavement

weeds that should have been removed
ages ago

don't worry little one

I've got you

you are safe now.

An Autopsy Of Us

An Autopsy Of Us

It feels like I have some
peach pit sized hole in my chest

it is big enough to ache
big enough that I notice the blood loss

but not large enough to be lethal

which is sometimes the worst part

it is big enough I feel incomplete
not big enough for others to notice

I can keep it hidden
beneath long sleeves
baggy sweaters

it is not enough for others to care

but it is enough
that I will never be the same.

I stick around because
it is easy
or easier to

when you think of life
not as a year
or a season

not as a decade
or a lifetime

but as starting with
the sunrise

and ending when it
sets

beginning with the breeze
and ending with the crashing of waves

I have lived many lives.

I think I have more in me.

1c Coffee
    Skimmed Milk
        Honey   0.31
1c Apple   1.04
2c Streamed Broccoli   0.60
1c Chicken Breast   1.65
1c Wild Rice   1.66
1c Carrots   0.32
1c Gum   0.04
2c Cookies   1.71
5c Water   0.00
                                              7.33

Discount Applied: *RUN*   -1.00

Total: *freedom*

An Autopsy Of Us

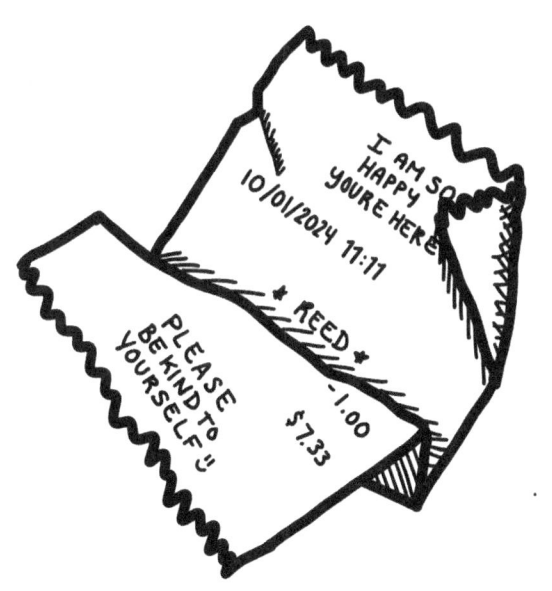

An Autopsy Of Us

Would you still love me
if I was a worm?

I don't ask under the assumption
that I will magically become a worm

when I ask that ridiculous question
I am really wondering

would you love me
if I was vulnerable?

if I were sick
would you leave me?

if you couldn't *have* my body
would you still hold it?

would you take extra caution
to not step on me in the rain

or would you leave me in the sun
to the birds and the shoes
of careless strangers not watching their step
because I was of no value anymore?

would you make me a little home
with dirt and berries

or release me into the wild
to be swallowed whole?

I know I am not a worm

but I fear I am nothing more
either.

Moss once told me
your ability to hold compassion
and empathy is astounding

I smiled

I know what she meant by that
what she wanted to say

you forgive too easily

you let people walk all over you and
say sorry that it made their feet hurt

I wear my empathy like
a bruised badge of honour

that sentence somehow made it feel worth it

but I smiled.

An Autopsy Of Us

I think Athena knew what she was doing
when she gave Medusa those snakes

the goddess of practical reason
worshipped by men
envied by women

one who had been shattered at the hands of men
and put herself back together

she would not blame another woman
for the criminal curiosity
the lawless lust of man

she would
however
know to keep their respect
she had to appease them

that men wouldn't see Poseidon for his
storming seas
and slimy hands

and so
a crown of serpents
the trojan horse of curses
trading beauty *to* men
for protection *from* them

and if Athena decided she was to be cursed
and left Medusa with those vipers out of
anger and spite

I would gladly receive a curse
from the hands of a woman

than the unwelcome touch
of a calloused man's.

An Autopsy Of Us

An Autopsy Of Us

Never in my life
has a man been content

not once have they accepted me

for what I am
what I offer willingly

I am accustomed to their
hungry eyes

seeing them long
for something I am not

a version of me that only exists
in their fantasies
and wet dreams

for once
in my fucking life

would you *see* me

instead of looking at me.

An Autopsy Of Us

We inherit more than
just the colour of our eyes

that trauma is passed down
like **a family heirloom**
a necklace of broken glass
worn around the neck
of each generation

i've inherited their fears
their wounds
the way they learned to hide
from love that looked too close

the way I swallow my pride instead of dinner
and measure my worth in crumbs and calories

I feel it
this weight
this lineage of scars that marks me
as part of a cycle I never asked to join

I want to rewrite the story

because I am more than I was given
because I've seen generations of women
succumb to the wolves and cry at the table

I will not be an heir to the ache

I will learn to exist without an apology
poised on my tongue

and my daughter and I will have dessert.

An Autopsy Of Us

I was a kid sitting with my legs dangled off the seat
I wasn't big enough to do my own seatbelt

but I was old enough
told enough times

that I needed to
suck in my stomach
eat less cake
dance for longer

I cried at the theme park
because I was scared I was too big for the rides

I wasn't.
I was five.
I was too *small* for half of the rides.

I stopped eating and danced harder
longer

I was the same chubby-cheeked kid but I was sick
I wished I was sicker.

give me a reason
I pleaded
to a man I didn't believe in
just take some weight
off of my shoulders
and my hips

I am 22 now

I will forever have a scar
halfway down my stomach

because from the age of 5
I was told to
suck it in.

An Autopsy Of Us

Aurora dances
across the sky

your arm around my shivering frame

we watch as she
changes colour

dances
through the wind

carrying with her ancient voices
and the secrets of those we lost

a tear escapes my eye

oh how I've missed you.

ah

the thing

as you so eloquently put it

I will say I am impressed

by your ability to find

simplicity
in chaos

the ability to wrap up *months*
of my agony

into a simple little package

into a neat and petite bundle

a short and sickly phrase to describe
how I gifted you a sacred piece of my flesh
and you to threw it to the dogs

I am jealous of how easily
you can sweep
our whole relationship under the rug

and pretend that I was the one
who betrayed you.

An Autopsy Of Us

Is my purpose to heal?

is my only job to mend everyone else
at my own expense?

will you always search for me
through cluttered bathroom drawers
and the bottom of your purse?

will you smile
and raise me in the air like a trophy
as if you worked tirelessly to earn me?

you will

they always do

you will take my advice
my warmth
my love

you will bleed onto me
until you are finished

once your cut is healed
and I still bleed out
you will discard me

because you no longer need me

i'm just a **bandage**.

An Autopsy Of Us

For you

I will drain every drop of water from the ocean
to find you the perfect shell

I will split an entire mountain range down the middle
if you want to see the core

I will hang each and every star
in a perfect constellation
of your smile
or freckles

just because

do you want the sun?
I will find a way to rip it from the sky
dooming all of us
dooming me

if you'd like

you don't even have to say **please**.

Your love is
a wilted rose

with thorns of resentment
and betrayal

once camouflaged by

delicate petals
and a sickly sweet scent

it is now a bare stem
stripped of its compassion

a poignant symbol

of lost love
and false hope.

An Autopsy Of Us

Your touch is a stain

you think it a joke
a prank
a harmless tickle

so meaningless I won't
bother to think of it again

bronze is beautiful
a signifier of wealth

in some cases

youth & innocence
in others

yet here I am
a tarnished statue
frozen in place

I started the shining copper
but became discoloured
building up protection from your
toxic air

you see beauty
bronze beneath your touch
you're impressed

meanwhile I see everything else

I am **oxidized** for my protection

only exposed because you
can't keep your hands
to yourself.

An Autopsy Of Us

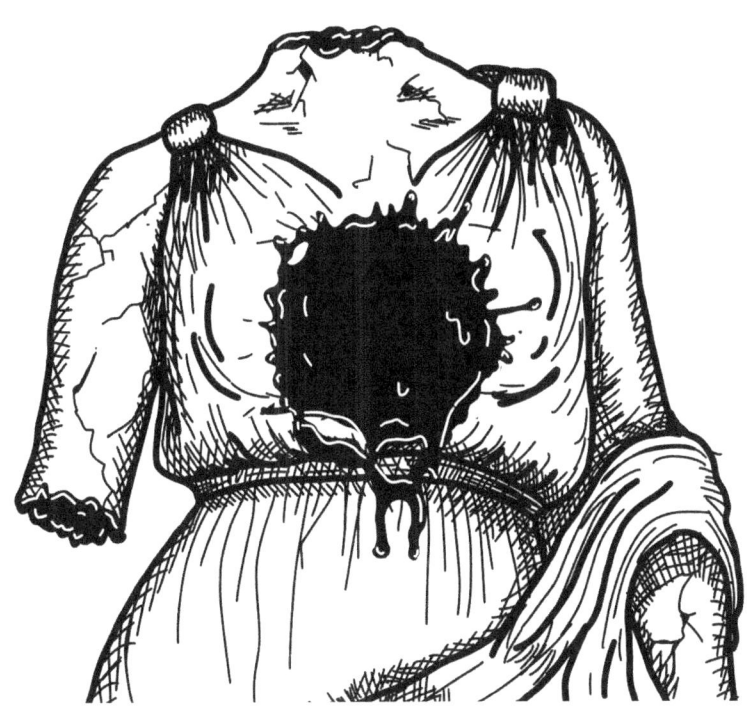

An Autopsy Of Us

Your apologies echo
through the hollow caves of us

colliding with the cold damp stone

roaring through the halls of
empty promises
and remorseless action

I know that a sorry from you
means as much as a smile
from a cougar

when you **anthropomorphize** something
humanize another species
reflect your emotion onto them

you see a smile
where there is a threat

and you get bit

hard

I know this to be true

but each and every time you come to me
teeth bare and body rigid

I don't brace for impact
against all of my better judgement

I smile
and let you back in

I think I will always let you back in

I hate myself for it.

An Autopsy Of Us

An Autopsy Of Us

we carve pumpkins
and leave them out
knowing they will rot

collect flowers
knowing that picking them
doomed them in the first place

and then water them
like a liquid apology will fix it

sometimes
fleeting moments
seem worth

the life lost

the relationship ended

I hope it was worth it

I hope **she** was worth it.

An Autopsy Of Us

I know I look stupid

picking at the scraps of you
calling it love

black and blue aren't really my colours
but if you think I should wear them
I will

I do

this isn't what love looks like
on the television
or in my books

but that is all fiction
and you are real
somehow

desperation has a funny way of turning
neglect into yearning

I dine on your distain
I savour each and every false promise

starving people will eat anything
and I

my dear

am ***famished***.

Your touch
once a gentle breeze

quickly morphed
into destructive winds
a hurricane

you left me a demolished landscape

once rich with trees
and flowers
and fauna

now a desolate field

empty and fractured

bare and broke.

An Autopsy Of Us

I would tell you I understand
what you did

or why you did it

but that would be a lie
and you know how I feel about liars

or maybe you don't

or maybe you did
once
but not anymore

it hurts less to think that you were just
blind to what you did

that my cries were simply landing
on **deaf ears**

and not those designed
specifically to hear anyone
but me.

I stick around in hopes that
like a flower in the spring

I will **bloom**

into something
new

something
beautiful

I don't.

but with each season
I find a new peace

in my own
petals.

An Autopsy Of Us

An Autopsy Of Us

You looked to me for salvation
but **I am not your saviour**

I cannot be

I am not here
to mend your broken pieces

to stitch together
the wounds
you refuse to heal

I have my own scars to tend to
my own battles to fight

and I cannot keep letting myself

bleed

to take care of you

because you refuse to.

These woods are not so enchanted
when you are running

fleeing

the oak trees stare with
beady eyes

and the willows weep

they reach out with their
gnarled fingers

and poison ivy

a maze of green and
distorted faces

though sometimes
fleeing is the only option

or at least the best one

and in that case
keep running

you may trip

you may fall

the branches will whip
and bruise

but you'll be free

and that
my dear
is worth so much more.

You haunt me
but not in the way people think

it's not the memories that linger
not your scent or your voice

it's the hunger
the gnawing
bottomless hunger
you left behind

you taught me to starve for love

now I can't tell the difference
between emptiness and desire.

An Autopsy Of Us

The biggest difference between us
now that it is all said and done
now that we are done

is that when they ask you
what happened?

you don't have to lie
when you say I left you

and I have the grace
the unearned respect
to lie

to defend you to all of my friends
and yours

who will never get a real answer
when they ask me
why?

An Autopsy Of Us

There was a moment
a single breath

where everything we built
began to crumble

it wasn't dramatic

no loud crash
no angry roar

Our last goodbye wasn't
marked by words

but by the silence that followed

in the way we stopped reaching out

how our hands fell to our sides
no longer searching for the other's

we parted
not with a bang

but with the softest whisper

of **what we used to be.**

An Autopsy Of Us

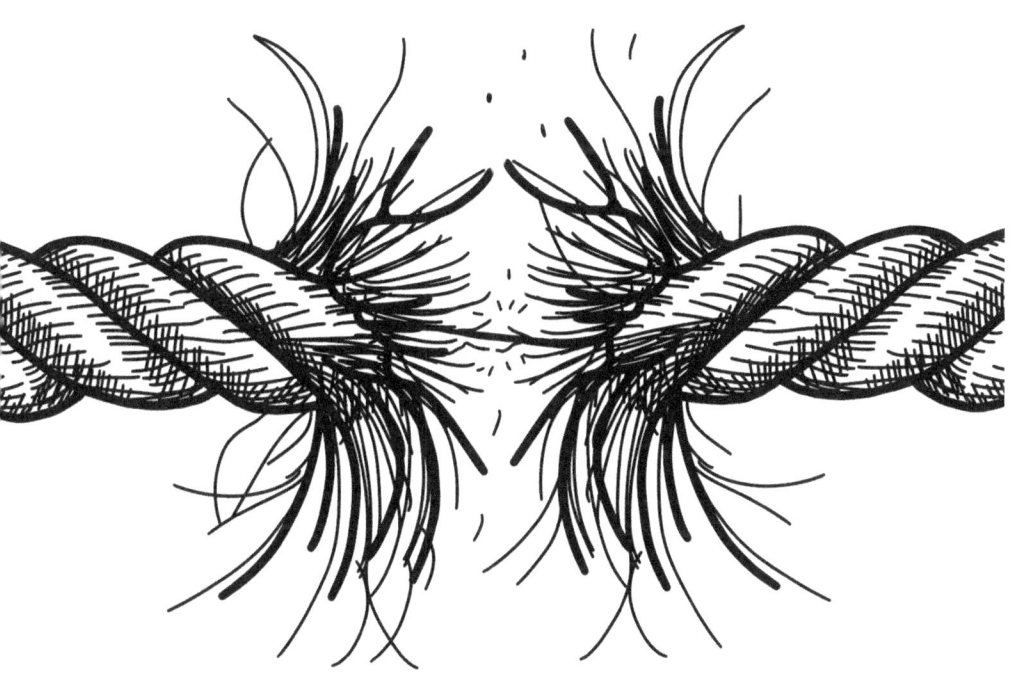

An Autopsy Of Us

We used to be whole

a single entity

but now we're **fragments**
scattered pieces of what once was

I hold these pieces in my hands

sometimes

wondering if they can ever
fit together again

or

if they were always meant
to fall apart.

An Autopsy Of Us

You left

I made you

but your ghost stays behind

lingering in the corners
of my mind

it whispers to me
in the dead of night
reminding me of the warmth
that once was

I try to exorcise you
to cleanse my heart of your presence

but **ghosts are stubborn** things

and you refuse to leave.

An Autopsy Of Us

I've searched for signs

scoured the texts
devoured the verses

hungry for a truth
any truth

the pages are barren
the fields salted

I have called into the night's sky
begged for mercy

for help

for a sign

the wolves call in mourning
sharing my sorrow

I called to you
your friends

any deity
who's name I could remember

silence.

An Autopsy Of Us

I wish I knew
letting go is not a single act

that I wouldn't wake up one day
and my chest would have stopped aching over night

letting go is a thousand little steps
I never thought I'd have to take

it's in the way I stop checking my phone
and how my heart no longer skips when it rings

in the way I am learning to sleep alone

and in the way I begin to find joy
in things that have nothing
to do with you

I still reach for you in my sleep sometimes
I can't help it

I used to panic
my eyes would fly open out of fear that
you weren't there because something bad happened

now when I feel the empty cold of our
my vacant sheets
on what I still call your side of the bed
I huff

oh

right

And hug myself a little tighter.

The **aftermath** is the hardest part

when the world moves on
but I'm still frozen
in that moment

replaying it over
and over
in my mind

the questions come like daggers
questions like
do you know what you did?
why was I the one consoling you?
why did you waste five years for five minutes?

some questions I cannot bring myself to ask

not even here

there are no answers
that can erase the shame

no words that can soothe
the burning guilt

that isn't mine to carry.

An Autopsy Of Us

**You didn't hit me
you didn't have to**

your hands
unwelcome and unforgiving
carved wounds deeper than any bruise

your entitlement
after years of *us*
was enough
to break the fragile trust I had
in you
in me
in the world

that a man would finally be nice to me

why couldn't you just stay nice to me?

you stole the safety I had
that I thought was finally mine

you ruined the one relationship I had
where I felt seen

you didn't raise your fist
or voice
but the damage is done

etched into my skin
my soul
carved into my bones
and my body

You didn't hit me
but you broke me all the same.

An Autopsy Of Us

I have written you
a thousand letters
in my mind

a thousand letters I will never send

each one filled with words I will never speak
and anger I fear I will always hold in my chest

they will sit
unwritten
at the edges of my consciousness
keeping me up at night

they will wait for courage that will never come

lucky you

you will never hurt the way I do
living in an ignorance I have
perfectly crafted to keep you

of all people

safe

I wish I had the love in me
to do that for myself.

In a **garden of one flower**

it is hard to find anything
worthy

of picking for your lover

of cultivating for next spring

of your last shot in a roll of film

in a world with no storms
it is hard to appreciate
the stillness of the sky
and the absence of the rain

in a world of storms
you will *always*
search for blue sky

so

in a garden
where all petals are alike
and all roots grow in unison

I am okay
being a weed.

An Autopsy Of Us

An Autopsy Of Us

I have dug through the rubble
searching for your **origin story**

every villain has one

they can be understood and pitied
can be reasoned with and swayed

as perverse as it may be
a villain has a goal or a purpose or a desire to pursue
driven by some twisted sense of justice

but you

you are something else entirely

what drives you is not something I can justify

it's not ambition not revenge not pain

i've tried to find the villain in the beast you've become

I *wanted* you to be one
to have some story that makes your actions forgivable
to believe in your redemption
even if I wouldn't be there to witness it

I never claimed to be a hero
but I refuse to be a martyr

I refuse to lay down my life
on your alter of nothingness

this is where I drop my armour and go home
no more will I beg for my peace

I refuse to be another casualty in
your endless war with yourself.

An Autopsy Of Us

I hope you know

now

that what you did
was an awful thing
to do to a person

even **someone like me.**

An Autopsy Of Us

I sink into **the water**
and I turn the heat up higher
hotter
until it scalds my skin

as if the burn could reach into the depths
of all the things I want to forget

I let the water consume me
hoping it can sear away the memories
the touch that somehow still lingers

I press deeper
feel the sting
and imagine it washing away
everything he left behind

as if the heat could purify
could cleanse the spaces
where his hands once were

I close my eyes
and pray for the pain to leave
for the water to carry it away

as if this bath could boil away all the darkness
leave me raw but clean

I am left with the realization
that some wounds run too deep
for water to reach.

An Autopsy Of Us

There's a fire beneath my skin
a quiet
simmering rage
lurking just below the surface

you can see it burn in my eyes
hiding in the shadows of my smile

the kind of anger that doesn't scream
or shout

it whispers in the night
filling my chest with heat
my veins with tension

it's the words I didn't say
the battles I chose not to fight

the injustices I swallowed whole
until they settled like stones
in the pit of my stomach

this anger isn't loud
it doesn't break things

it festers

like a wound left untended
slowly poisoning me

and though I try to keep it buried
to push it down
it rises

like smoke from a smouldering home
a reminder that beneath this surface
I am **still burning**.

I would be a lot happier
if I didn't think about

the things that I cannot change
the words that left my lips too soon
or the chances that I didn't take

if I didn't think of
the pinkies that would be broken
if swearing meant anything

if I didn't think
about the what-ifs and maybes

if I didn't think
of the could-have-beens and might-have-beens

if I didn't think
or the dreams that never came true

if I didn't think

if I didn't think

If I didn't think.

An Autopsy Of Us

I have carried **the weight of almost**
deep in my chest
an ache that settles in the spaces
between breaths

a quiet reminder of what nearly was
of the love that danced just out of reach
teasing me with possibilities
that never found their way to me

you were almost mine
a dream I could almost touch
something I could almost believe in

and I was almost enough to make you stay
almost the one

but almost is a heavy word
a promise that never quite took shape
a love that lingered on the edges
hovered in the doorway
never stepping fully in

I almost reached for you
almost said the words that burned on my lips
almost let you see the parts of me I kept hidden
the wounds and the wishes

but we stayed there
on the brink of something we couldn't quite name
almost brave almost ready

we are the ones who came close but never arrived
we are the ghosts of our own undone decisions

almost is not enough
so we let the almosts pile up

but endless stacks of nothing is still empty space.

An Autopsy Of Us

Don't tell me *it was **meant to happen***
as if pain is preordained
as if every tear I've shed
was written in some celestial script

as if the ache in my chest
is just part of a grander plan
written in the stars long before I drew breath

don't whisper to me about fate
about how everything happens for a reason
as if that makes it easier to swallow
the bitterness of losing myself

how can you say it was meant to be
when the nights are long
and the days are hollow
when the dreams I held so tightly
slipped through my fingers
leaving nothing but the sting of their absence?

there's no comfort in your words
no solace in the idea
that my suffering was somehow necessary
that it had to happen
so I could learn
so I could grow

No.

I found my own way
through the wreckage
not because it was destined
but because I had no choice
but to survive.

An Autopsy Of Us

It's strange to go back
to walk the streets
that used to be home

where every corner held a memory
a piece of who I was

the things I loved about my hometown
are mostly gone now

Moss moved across the country
taking our laughter and late-night talks with her

and the blue dog cafe
the one that saved my life
with its warm light and quiet corners
closed its doors
like a final chapter in a book
I wasn't ready to finish

It feels like visiting a ghost town
where the echoes of who I used to be
linger in the air

it's not the same
and maybe that's why it feels so strange

to stand in the midst of what was
and realize that time moves on

that **this place is not the same**
and neither am I.

An Autopsy Of Us

There is a **phantom limb**
where my hope used to be

I still reach for it sometimes
expecting to feel the pulse
of something alive beneath the skin

But all I find is emptiness

a hollow cavity where I once kept dreams
Now a graveyard of what-ifs

and I visit it like a tomb

I bring flowers every night
arrange them in the shape of the life
we almost had
I almost had

They rot faster each time.

When the smoke clears
and the embers fade to black
I will see the truth

bare and unforgiving
like the bones of a forest
stripped by fire

I once danced in those flames
thinking they were light
believing that the heat
was just another name for love

I know now
the blaze was only ever meant to consume me

in the aftermath
I walk through the wreckage
each step a reminder of what I lost
and what I've gained

the air is thick with the memory
but I no longer choke on it

when the smoke clears
I see the ruins of what we built

and i'll know it was never a home
just a place we burned
to distract from the cold

when the smoke clears
the truth will hang in the air
thick and undeniable

I'll realize that the only thing lost
was the illusion
and what's left is the truth.

An Autopsy Of Us

You are the bottle of ink
spilled upon my pages

to you
only a few drops are missing from the bottle

a bottle easily replaced
replenished

I am the pages

your stain soaking into my fibres
leaving your mark

An Autopsy Of Us

your stain
        on each

An Autopsy Of Us

                    and every
                          sheet

                                  Or

An Autopsy Of Us

almost.

An Autopsy Of Us

I have built altars in your name
sculpted from every doubt I swallowed
every tear I hid

I became your advocate
crafting tales of your goodness
to anyone who questioned you

convincing myself that
I wasn't just another fool
with a heart too big for someone so small

today I lay down my sword
I will no longer stand there
at the gates of your crumbling castle
guarding a ruin I mistook for a home

you were a lesson I had to learn the hard way
but I am done being a student of your cruelty
a scholar of your deceit

consider this my final contribution
the moment I step away
the moment I stop lighting candles
to chase away the shadows you left behind

here it is
the last piece of me you'll ever take
or hold
or touch
a page you may never see
or will rip apart if you do

where I say

I am so fucking sorry

not to you
but to myself.

An Autopsy Of Us

An Autopsy Of Us

Hey you!

Thank you for taking the time to journey through these pages with me. Writing has always been my way of making sense of the world, of navigating the chaos and finding meaning in the midst of pain. My words are a reflection of my experiences, my struggles, and my hopes. They are an outpouring of emotions that, at times, felt too heavy to carry alone.

I write because I believe in the power of storytelling to heal, to connect, and to empower. To share the parts of myself that are often hiding behind a well-timed joke or a carefully crafted sentence.

I am only 23, but I believe I have a lot to say. With this book, I wanted to try something different. I chose to leave these poems unpolished and raw, capturing them in their most authentic form. These poems are like my thoughts at 3 a.m. —unfiltered and messy, but deeply raw, honest, and possibly *too* personal. All written during a time where I was unsure how to survive leaving an abusive, long term relationship. At times I felt that staying would be easier than re-learning how to be on my own.

If you read through this collection and related, I am deeply sorry. You deserved better and I promise you it is coming.

If you're sitting there after reading and thinking, '*Could this be about me?*' It's never too late to work on yourself, Parker. Therapy is a great place to start. ♥

With peace, love, and gratitude,

D. Leighton

www.ingramcontent.com/pod-product-compliance
Lightning Source LLC
Chambersburg PA
CBHW071253070526
44583CB00017B/2453